Eve

Jacinta Secker

BookLeaf Publishing

Presentation by *BookLeaf Publishing*

Web: www.bookleafpub.com

E-mail: info@bookleafpub.com

ISBN: 9789357211758

First edition 2023

DEDICATION

To my Daughters

ACKNOWLEDGEMENT

Firstly, I would like to thank my good friend from high school, Alex Obrien, for sending me the link to the BookLeaf Publishing 21 day poetry writing challenge. As a busy mother, I would have never known about this challenge so thank you for taking the time to inform me and for remembering my love for creative writing! I also want to thank my parents for encouraging me to pursue an interest in literature, to my husband for supporting me through this challenge, and all friends and family that supported me as well. I want to thank all the strong inspiring women in my life who have inspired many of the themes in my creative writing and who have made me the person I am today. Lastly, I would like to thank BookLeaf Publishing for renewing my creative spirit through their TheWriteAngle poetry challenge and for allowing me this opportunity to showcase my creative work.

Eve

Eve

The woman who brought
humanity to it's knees,
Supposedly I'm your daughter

Eve

A daughter of Eve,
Beguiled every time
I defy a man as you did

Eve

Taking a bite
from the forbidden tree,
The sweetness,
The Desire,
How dare we!

Eve

Your one act of defiance
put all us women on our knees,
Sitting in pain as we bleed and scream,
Bringing forth more daughters of

Eve

Desire

I feared it once,
Wouldn't let myself feel it,
Tried to push the thought of sin
Somewhere outside of this....

Heart of mine,
That was yearning to feel,
What it was to desire,
I didn't know it would heal...

My sense of self,
Give me direction,
And clarity,
I learned who I was,
When I let desire carry me...

It took the gentle caress of a hand,
A guidance and dance of lips,
A seductive grin,
A wild smile,
A toss of care,
Throwing myself into thin air,
Letting desire guide me to the floor,
In a warm embrace,
Forgetting all I had been taught,

And accepting my fate...

I desire freedom,
Not fear,
Knowing what I want is not a bad thing,
Desire is something I need not fear.

Cold

Seeping
Creeping
Into your pores,
Through your veins,
Slowing motion,
Body shakes,
Longing for homeostasis,

Liquid pours
Out of eyes,
Nose,
Throat,
Freezes onto skin
Turning it red,
Icy fire on flesh
A pain without death,

White fire
Riding on the wind,
Rearing in your face,
Burying itself into your eyes,
Seeking out your demise.

All I Want For Christmas Is Sleep

Sleep
To rest my head
My eyes
My soul
To slip into dreams
Filled with peace
No heartaches
No woes,

Alas!
Midnight shift calls
Soothe my children
Soothe my man
Sink into fits of anxiety
Instead of dreams
Santa all I want for Christmas
Is some sleep!

Sleep
So I feel that I have a brain cell again
To walk a little straighter
Smile a little brighter
To be the best Mom I can be
Is it really too much to ask for some sleep?!

Even several hours
Where I don't wake up in bed
Thinking of a million things
I need to do In my head
To have no more anxiety dreams
To wake up feeling refreshed and relieved,

Santa
All I ask for this Christmas is some good sleep!

Where is My Village?!!

Where is my village?!!
I lay crumbled on the floor,
Heartbeat increases more,
My spirit is poor,
I cover my ears,
Fighting off tears,
My child screams in my ears,
Why is it only me?
Expected to care for this being?
To do everything?!

Where is my village?!!

I can't do everything!
I can barely care for me!
I'm so tired I can hardly see!
My child needs more then my love,
She needs stronger hugs,
From people not crumbling into dust,

Where is my village?!!

Someone hear me please,
As I join in with her screams,
I don't want to plead,

But I'm Punching the wall,
Feeling myself fall,
Starring blankly down the hall,
Motherhood is crippling,
Mood is swinging,
I'm barely clinging,

Where is my village?!!

Grandma's, Grandpa's,
Aunts, and uncles too!
Where are you?!
Friends, coworkers,
Neighbours, cousins,
Community too!
Where are you?!
You said you would be here,
You said that you cared!

Now daughter and I sit alone,
Holding each other in this cold,
Hold and trusting that each other is enough,
Yet wondering.....

Where is our village?!

Appetizing Fire

Your fire is appetizing
Watching you swing
Into motion
No fear of anything
Who would want a submissive partner?!
Not me!
Living with you is never boring,

You don't take no for an answer
I press buttons
And you go on fire
You're wild
And a little crazy
But honestly,
You are my everything!

I dance around your glow
Starring into eyes full of hope
With you by my side
Shining like a light
I will never grow old,

Your fire is appetizing!

You are so bold
Your fire will forever glow.

Ghosts in the Fog

There is something peaceful
About early morning fog,
Waking up to a thick blanket of cold
Smothering all sounds
Other then the fog horn
Ringing loud
Sounding from the port,
The salty breeze carry's it to my ears
It's all I can hear
As I sip my morning coffee
Wondering what lays under
This thick blanket of fog.

I imagine my ancestors
Dancing in the grey
Calling to me softly
To come out and play!
It's haunting
This field
All covered in fog,
If I stepped out
I'd get lost in their song!
I think of the spirits
Who hide in this haze
The trail blazer,

Wander,
Lost child,
The witches, wizards,
And old hags,
What did they find
As they wander this mist?
The purpose of life
Or the answer to their wish?

The fog starts to lift
Fresh dew sits in the trees,
It sparkles like diamonds
As the sun touches the leaves,
It's a new day
The ghosts disappear
As did my coffee
I'm sad to share,
I go out into the world today
Toil on the land
Where my ancestors played,
I sing their song
Honour their work
By sticking my hands
in the dew soft dirt,
I dream of tomorrow
When again I might see
The ghosts in the fog
Smiling at me!

Two Coffee Mugs

Two coffee mugs
Treated with care
Pottered by their maker
To be a pair

Once they were held
In lover's hands
While they snuggled together
Conversing about foreign lands

The mugs
They complemented each other
They were crafted different
But meant to be together
The women who held one
Believed the same
Her and the man
Were meant to be this way

To be different
But together
Complementing the other
To sit on the counter in warm embrace
To hold hands together
For the rest of their days

Now she holds one mug
And stares at the other
Weeps tears of pain
Both mugs remain
But one is shattered

Any Flower

Roses are red
Violets are blue
No one out there
Is as unique as you!

You might be a Daisy
White as the snow
You might be a Dandelion
Dirty yellow but cool

Or maybe you are a Forget Me Not,
Blue as the sky
Or a Daffodil
Old and wise

Or possibly a Crocus
The first to rise
Or a Sunflower
High in the sky

Or a Tulip
Bright and sleek
Or a Water Lily
Down where the animals drink

You can be any size
Shape or form…

Roses are red
Violets are blue
But you,
You can be anything you choose!

Phases

In my dreams
I could see life spilt into three,
Three phases one must pass
To find peace that would last.

The first was the one
We dream of all the time,
To own, to control materials and lives,
Everything from books, games and TV's,
Motor homes, cars, and SUVs,
From jewels to pearls, clothes and attire,
To having staff, maids, and squires.

I stood between this phase and the next,
Shaking to see what must come to pass,
To be totally, utterly, completely free!
The second phase
Was to loose everything….

I stood at the gate crying with grief,
I didn't want to leave the things
I thought I would need,
Yet I also could see
Standing in this thin veil,
Those who didn't leave that phase

Where held down and pale,
Trapped and imprisoned
By things they held dear,
To stay in that place
Was my greatest fear!

I left for the nothing
The wild,
The storm,
Each step was torture
My heart was so worn,
The nothingness took all the life within me
Till I became nothing but a vessel at sea,
In a sea of emptiness
Bitter it was,
But the beauty was gorgeous
Even when glum!
The sun was bold,
The nights dark and grey,
The cold air carved marks
In my face like waves,

I don't know how long
I wandered that land
Of nothing and harshness,
Bitter yet bland,
I wandered till all that was left in me
was an acceptance
that there is something greater then me,

When I entered the third phase
I smiled with relief,
My empty vessel
Was now full of things!
I found on this side
As I lay in the grass,
The things that didn't own me
But instead made up the best....

The best parts of who I am,
I rest in this peace,
Feeling a soft breeze
Content with nothing,
Grateful for my personality
Crafted by going through
The three phases of being.

Motherhood

Mother
Overwhelmed
Tired
Heart
Enthusiasm
Rewarding
Hard
Overthinking
Odd
Devoted

The Brightest Star

Laughter,
Song, skipping, dance,
All come halting in a crash!
Her loud booming voice
Chases down memory lane,
Her dark cheerful eyes,
Go still.....the car crashes,
A future that would have been bright
With more laughter, children, and delight!
Is laid still in the grave.

Looking into her eyes,
As us twelve year olds played,
Would never have guessed,
She would end this way!
What a way to start a year,
When one of the brightest stars disappears....

At the same time you're glad
She escaped the cruel nip of life,
The betrayals, the pain,
The cold sleepless nights,

Yet at the core she reminds you
You never know the time,

You might be healthy like she was,
But death comes to all in time.

So pick up your life!
For short it might be,
Hold onto the ones you love,
Before they are no longer seen.

The Sea and the Shore

I stand by an ocean,
The waves lap against my legs,
The breeze blows my hair,
I stand in the sun
Not the shade,

The sun bakes my frame,
Darkens my eyes,
But the sea is cooling,
Intelligent and wise,

I see my reflection,
Strong, hardened,
Cold,
Is it like the sun
Fiery and hard,
Or like the moon
Distant and cool?

I suppose it's a bit of both!
Fiery but distant,
Hot yet cold,
Balanced,
In tune,
Hurting yet bold,

Waves chip away the hardness,
Life flows under the water,
And although I still stand
hardened on shore,
Step by step,
Every groan, cry, and laugh,
I will emerge myself in the waves,
And fear no more.

Dreams

All are born
With dreams in their head,
Imaginations of incredible worth!
Ideas that could change the world,
Inventions that would blow one's mind,
But then something happens....
The dream withers and dies.

The incredible things that would happen
If dreams never died,
More smiles we would see,
More joy and bliss there would be,
More hope, achievements, and glee!
If dreams never died.

How dare one stifle a dream!
Do you not realize successful nations
Are built off dreams?!
They are built of visions, ideas,
Realistic or not,
Creations, passions, imagination,
And thought.

Dreams have enough opposition,
So your voice doesn't have to be one too,

Your voice might be the one little thing
That makes a dream come true!

Star Crossed Lovers

There is no plausible way
We can be together!

It breaks my heart...

I see you in my mind
Standing on the porch,
You rest your hands on my hips,
I rest my hands on your heart,

Star crossed lovers…

It's too freakishly true!
All I want is to be with you!
What is this madness taken over my soul?!
There is no logic in my love towards you,
I would have to give up everything
To be with you!
I told myself
I would never feel this way,

Yet here I am…..

Pouring my heart out
Onto the page.

I don’t know when
I will see you again,
If I ever will,
My heart continues to break,
Hoping I can either move on
from this pain,
Or be in your arms again!

Dying World

I see a world
Starting to die!

Creation crumbling
Under manufactured waste,
Plastics constricting airways,
Poison in life giving water,
Smog to darken the day.

Children can no longer
Sit in a classroom and feel safe!
They enter walls
Supposed to be refuge,
Hoping not to see
A gun in their face!

The Earth shatters
With our impact on it,
Crying out with volcanoes,
Earthquakes,
And giant waves!
How long will it take
Till she truly cracks and breaks?!

The world is dying,

I want to cry,
For so much beauty
Is still left to find,
Yet all things come,
And all things go,
The reason why God only knows!

It's a dying world,
I feel it in my bones,
But I still cling on
To a little hope,
That we change our ways,
That time pauses on a dime,
That this now broken world
Once again,
Becomes paradise.

Deconstructing Faith

Where has my faith gone?!
I ask myself this all the time!
I used to be so pious once,
I would have given my life
For Christ!

What changed?
How did something so strong
Fade away?
Did the devil get inside my brain?

I prayed!
Night and day,
For strength
To resist temptations
That came my way!
And I stayed pure,
Holy and chaste!

Fear,
I was tired of living in fear,
If God truly loved me,
Then why was there so much
For me to fear!?!
Why was hell thrown in my face

Every time I was a disgrace?
So I was labeled,
For showing a little skin,
Speaking out,
Or being too able!
Called a devil,
Selfish,
Ungrateful.

Yet men were able,
To stick their hands down
Our backs,
And only get a little slap,
Hush, hush,
That's just how men are,
Maybe your skirt should
Go down longer by far!
Or maybe you asked for it?!
Even though you didn't
Know what you were asking for!
We keep you uneducated,
So you don't look for more,

And if you do,
We call you worldly,
Drawn to the pleasures of this life,
We teach you to accept pain,
So that when it happens
You smile in it's face,

Not looking for a way to escape,
To a place that would be
Better for you!

Sounds awful
Right?!
And yet every single night,
I still question if I was right?!
Or if I am like Eve,
Eating the fruit from the forbidden tree,
Thinking it will be good for me,
But maybe I'm deceived?!

No One Cares

No one cares,
No one seems to dance at my ideas,
Or care to hear what I have to say,
Or the thoughts in my head,
The things I love,
I love alone,
When they die,
I cry alone.
No one cares,
Unless value it has
In others eyes,
Otherwise,
These thoughts, feelings,
Emotions, troubles,
Heartaches,
Joys,
Excitement,
Are cared for only by me.

Even those who say they love me
Can't emphasize,
Unless value they see inside,
Otherwise,
I sit with all these visions in my head,
These thoughts,

These dreams,
To others dead.
And if I shared that I feel alone,
Others would they say
I just moan and groan?
Tears in my eyes,
The weight of my cares
On me lies,
To carry on this lonely road,
Where no one cares,
And I'm all alone.

The Land

I belong to the land,
Born on its soil,
Where I work and Toil,
A part of the landscape,
My rugged frame,
Beat down by the sun,
During the day,
Dry and cracked
Like the earth,
Where I dig in the dirt,
Planting tree after tree,
As my fingers hurt.

My ancestors
They worked this land,
Then they raped this land,
And I try to restore it again,
The Earth is not gentle,
And it isn't kind,
Like it remembers
Us pulling out its roots
and it's vines,
So new vines it grows
To trip my toes,
And toss me into rocks,

Leaving me battered and shocked,
But in awe of the wildness
Stretched before my eyes,
Of the valleys and mountains
Reaching up for the sky.

And despite how being on the Earth
Makes me age,
Cuts the smoothness from my skin,
Leaving grooves and little graves,
I can't help but marvel
At the beauty of it all,
How it leaves me breathless,
And totally in awe!
It gives back to me,
Despite twigs snapping in my face,
The land doesn't forget,
But it has grace!
And the more I grow
Connected to this land,
The less pain I feel,
The more I understand,
The land changes,
But it doesn't die,
More people will walk it's face,
Who are young and spry,
We will leave our mark on it,
And it on you and me,
The past and present

One in the moment,
Existing through the land,
This I now see.

Women

Women are beautiful,
Yet stubborn as a donkey,
Their mind is their own!

Silence

Oh beautiful silence!
I sit in the quiet,
Away from the hustle and bustle
Of the day,
I'm always needed,
I'm always wanted,
It's hard to sneak away,
To this place of refuge
That I know,
Where I can finally be alone,
Welcome the heavy cloak of no sound,
Sitting in the temple of myself.

In the silence I feel the pain
Of many many yesterdays!
Of all the years that I've known,
Of my time back at home,
Where I grew up
And was taught to be
A version of a lady
That wasn't me!
I still feel that hurt today,
But I now understand the pain,
And the silence helps me learn to forgive,
And to unlearn past sins,

In this darkness I find myself,
A tiny child who needed help,
And I take her by the hand,
To go off to far better lands,
Where she can be herself again!

In this dome of peace,
I think of all my possibilities,
All the places I might go,
If I hold onto Hope,
Days may be dark and grim,
But I am sure to win,
For power in me
Lies within,
A lioness,
Putting on her armour
In the silence of this hour.

www.ingramcontent.com/pod-product-compliance
Lightning Source LLC
Chambersburg PA
CBHW051742130826
49812CB00033B/961
9789357211758